Festival of Dangerous Ideas

Lenny DellaRocca

Festi of Danger

val
ous
IDEAS

Lenny DellaRocca

Published by Unsolicited Press
www.unsolicitedpress.com

Copyright © 2019 Lenny DellaRocca

All Rights Reserved.

No part of this book may be reproduced or transmitted in any form or by any means without written permission from the publisher or author.

Editor: S.R. Stewart
Cover Art: Eleanor Adair (https://eleanoradair.com)

For information, contact publisher at info@unsolicitedpress.com

Unsolicited Press Books are distributed to the trade by Ingram. Printed in the United States of America.
ISBN: 978-1-947021-60-0

Thanks to Bruce Weber, Michael Mackin O'Mara, Peter Hargatai, George Wallace, Gary Kay, Meryl Stratford, Sally Naylor, Barbra Nightingale, Stacie M. Kiner, Deborah DeNicola, Linda Avila, Paul Saluk, Susannah Simpson, Patricia Whiting, Lori Schainuck and Stephen Schaurer for their invaluable advice and suggestions.

And always, for Marie, for being there.

Contents

Festival of Dangerous Ideas	3
Neo	5
The Sleep Talker	7
Mr. Zootageek	8
Consuelo Maldonado Returns	9
Geppetto's Smile	10
Man Who Teaches Children to Fly	11
Lost Boy	12
Escape	14
Vague Symbols	16
Beginning of Daydreams	17
Strangers in a Grove	19
Library of Imaginary Books	21
History of the Invisible Child	22
Story of the Invisible Child	23
Touch of the Invisible Child	24
Twilight's Grove	25
After the Twining	27
Saints of Electrocution	28
The Meeting	29
The Patriot	30
After the Blast	31
Alphabetical Disorder	32
The New Language	33
Done in Chalk	34
Tower of Myth	35
Birth of Myth	36
Click	37
Blueprints	38
Gorgeous	40
Spice	41
Don't Blink	42

Spark's Shadow	43
Oboe	44
Evening of Metronomes	45
Revenge of the Genie	46
Revenge of the Atheist	47
Tea for One	48
The Colony	49
Static from Heaven	50
Mirror People	52
Girl Who Gets Gifts from Birds	53
Aunt Angelina's Prophecy	54
The Contraption	56
The Machine	57
The Box	58
The Town	59
The Girl on the Roof	60
Lady in the Yellow Summer Dress	61
Catching Angels	62
Angel's Song	63
Rain	64
Windows	65
Notes	67
Acknowledgements	72
About the Author	75
About the Press	76

Festival of Dangerous Ideas

Festival of Dangerous Ideas

A boy walks through a rusted gate
on the other side of the tracks
in a part of the world
that was not here yesterday.
A thirty-foot burning man of straw
blows smoke rings at a quarter moon.
Pigs with fiddles play bluegrass.
Banners proclaim anti-gravity potions on sale
and Aunt Angelina, *The Italian Gypsy,*
lays out a cross of cards for acrobats
and magicians.
On a dirt path ahead he finds a wooden box
with a singing man inside.
He shakes the box silencing his father.
Libraries burn in a square past
the Ferris wheel.
Poets wipe foreheads with ashes
of dead languages.
Further down- red meat, heads and limbs of dolls.
Crows alight from a theater of silent film.
Moon-side of a cotton candy concession
Marco Polo barks the show is about to begin,
points to the opera house made of ivory
and aircraft wreckage.
On stage an old man juggles
burnt dictionaries,
shards of the periodic table of elements,
the head of a senator…

Neo

Gradually, we began to call things
by new names,
the hard pronunciations of new tongues.
As if one day the sun rose over
California and we threw our shadows
oddly on the ground.
Awkwardly, we conversed with those
who drove the 18-wheelers, the tractors,
those who sold bread.
But we stopped calling it bread.
It was another name and its taste
eventually changed so that it too
became new.
After a while, no one noticed how differently
we spoke, how many words vanished,
replaced by a handful of new words,
difficult to make, our mouths not used to
the strange new shapes,
the throat a little sore from such rasping.
The books our children read
became more alien with each chapter
until by the end, nothing in them
was in our language.
And while most have forgotten,
some of us remember, we say them
in dreams,
over and over, so as not to forget them,
pronouncing them very carefully
so that we don't change a vowel,
preserve each inflection like our last breath.
Each night a different set of old words,
their meaning and history

5

so that one day we can say them
again, to others, outside.

The Sleep Talker

Sometimes the only thing in the world
is a crisp day and a train
where in one window
an old professor dreams of the one equation
that unites zero gravity with summer light
so that everything anyone
could ever wish for becomes real.

Space is his blackboard
on which he writes with the chalk of moons:
*I see myself in the shock-work of quarks,
in the dizzy twirl of stars.*

He dreams he is a boy
with a girl in the woods
sprinkling breadcrumbs behind them,
a man in Vienna
making a puppet out of wood
that will someday fall in love.

I warm my hands around that cup
and close my eyes... Hear that?

Mr. Zootageek

I go out under the moon,
plant seeds in my neighbor's back yard.
He is getting on in years.
I only know him by a wave of his hand
from across the fence at twilight,
when he walks in his gardens smoking a pipe
redolent with cherries.

Sometimes I find a wicker basket
of white eggplant or summer squash
under a quilted cloth on my front stoop.
It's from him, Mr. Zootageek,
that's what I call him,
named after an old magician
I read about in a newspaper.

He calls doves from the sky, and girls faint, the paper said.

He's older now, believes the pumpkins I've planted
appear in the dirt like magic.
Birds from all over the neighborhood
sing all night on the fence between our yards.
It is a ceremony of crows
in a back yard that goes on forever.

Consuelo Maldonado Returns

I wake up.

Something glows on the floor—

footprints of an angel.
Look out my bedroom window.
A train swims across the lawn.
A girl in one of the windows
waves at me. I wave back.
I remember her.
She sat next to me in English.
Her hair was a black town underwater.
She says, *Have you ever asked*
the full moon for change of a dollar?
It's why stars twinkle like dimes,
why men fall in love with angels.

I wake up.

Geppetto's Smile

My father makes my face from wet stone rubbed
with indigo.

A few light years for the eyes, he says, *teeth chipped from a pugilist.*

He puts a sparrow in my mouth,
teaspoon of lithium. I dream about a girl made of balsa.

I am blue veins made from worms
from the back yard after a hail storm.

I blink an afterlife.

The distance from my bedroom window
to the morning star is measured with a poem.

Kirkegarde, my father mumbles,
existential liar!
I am almost done.

Give me twilight, I tell my maker, *some wilderness and gold.*

A wristwatch at the open door in my chest.

Tick. Tick.

Man Who Teaches Children to Fly

I am making a man from clicks of light, a man with a voice
only a child can hear.

Making him out of footprints in snow, shimmering
        puddles in the woods, from a dusty floor
of a house nobody lives in.

When the stars come out I give him tea with bergamot and
lime, tell him to step into their dreams,

show them how to lift from the ground,
how to float above trees all over the world.

Each morning
children floating toward the sun.

Lost Boy

You create cinema, poetry,
but one of them is stuck in your head.

You see things, try to tell friends
but they give you that Look.
So when you splice
The Secret Life of Walter Mitty
with *Do Not Go Gentle into That Goodnight,*
nobody invites you for coffee anymore.

You can't tell them you see Cinderella
making love to Rodney Dangerfield.
But would you tell them you saw
the other side of the moon
because of that night with Peter Pan?

You've heard folks ridiculed after
claiming abduction by creatures
with obsidian eyes,
beamed up to a ship.
Have you ever told anyone
about the woman who appeared
when you were four,
hovered above the grass
on the other side of the fence
in your back yard,
clean in the light of pearls?

Now put your hand in your pocket.

That old dusty star burns your thumb.
Throw it into a well, watch it disappear.

Wish.

Escape

A boy wanders through a museum
reading titles of art—
Headless Bees of Ecuador,
wonders where the heads are,
are they pinned to a corkboard,
were they fed to parrots?

Colony I
reminds him of a film—
scientists living three years
in a secret domed complex in the desert
studying ants.
But the ants were studying them.
When the scientists tried to escape,
the ants cut the electricity.

He loves *Jackrabbit Cellar*—
imagines rabbits reading books,
eating carrots in arm chairs,
and little yellow lamps on end tables
where they tap cigars in ashtrays
read newspapers, and
The Illustrated Man, Atlas Shrugged.

Shadow Chord
reminds him of a dream—
movie star in a nightgown
playing piano under the Eiffel Tower
in the snow.

The boy faints behind a docent
who points to a collage
of photographs of his family
behind a barbed wire fence titled
You Are Here.

Vague Symbols

It chants in a crowd of chairs,
sarcastic, fine, tenacious.

It yelps from a fire escape,
wet, corrosive, stoic.

It defends grief in public,
draped in lavender, wicked.

It passes judgment on art,
forgetful, formal, smitten by women.

It casts its shadow in the air,
doleful, chrome-plated, tangible.

It bends light with a sleepy finger,
backward, starry, *loco*.

Beginning of Daydreams

After a special commemorative edition of *Life The Wizard of Oz, 75 Years Along the Yellow Brick Road*

My sister takes me to a neighbor's house to watch a film. I'm bewitched by a weather vane,

a song that stays in my head for the rest of my life, and a white lie swirling

in a milky crystal ball. A sinister column of air howling with all the blackness

in a green woman's heart sizzles the ground. A house tumbles from the sky,

a girl opens the door clutching her basket, her little dog too. She steps outside.

Who cannot recite word for word what she says? And then she dances across

the screen battling witches, flying monkeys, angry apple trees only to go home,

slop hogs, walk atop fences, sleep in a small wooden room. What is she thinking?

Stay in Oz silly girl, hide those slippers in a field of poppies. Grab the Tin Man's ax and cut the ropes of that runaway balloon, tell that ridiculous woman in the bubble

you're not going home.

Strangers in a Grove

On your way to work you see a sign posted
in an old orange grove,

Coming Soon: New Theater of Performing Arts called
Once Upon a Time.

A jester already waits for a job,
bells a-jangle on his cap;

a woman with blue hair wears a Venetian mask;

bare-breasted dwarf stands on his head;

something with wings balances an umbrella on its nose;

a Lollipop Girl stands at an easel
sketching birds in the eyes of witches.

You realize you're humming
"Somewhere Over the Rainbow".

How long before this turns dangerous?

Pilings go up, bulldozers overturn mounds
of earth once blazing with fruit.

A hundred trees piled under a blue,
suburban sky.

The actors wear necklaces of leaves,
twigs in hair.

Get out of your car.

You mustn't do this,
but you've seen them before.
They approach you, call your name,
but not the name you had
when you left home.

A week goes by, a year.
Your husband puts flyers on telephone poles
all over town.
They are fading.

He stops. Gets out of his car,
his shoes click on the walkway
leading to the door
of the theater he can barely see.
He becomes more and more
transparent with each step
until the ruby slippers on your feet
sparkle brighter than the sun.

You vanish right before his eyes.

Library of Imaginary Books

Long corridors lit with gas lamps.
With each step you see books
roiling out of dust,
books written by sailors not yet born,
jugglers from before the stars
turned on their lights,
books by granddaughters of wise-women
who burned at the stake.

Which title will you choose?
The Girl with Lavender Wings
or *The Elephant Who Plays Violin?*
They are written in a language
that glows in the dark.
Characters parade in circus down hills
that do not belong in this world.

Spend a few minutes in library time
and years will pass.
Will you give up everything?
Will you stay with the blind astronomer,
the black princess of China?

Sit on the bench by the water fountain
teeming with birds. Never grow up.
Never leave.

History of the Invisible Child

Fall asleep in a library overnight
which in library time is ages
because a book is like a child
waiting to grow up.

You are a child
curled in the dark chocolate of history
among proverbs and calculus,
inhaling passages
from oracles and thieves.
The world could end here
as it has many times.
But not now,
not while you sleep-walk
among old knowledge.

Lift objects with a thought,
speak to the dead,
blossom in pentameters of rhyme.

What if you never wake?

Someone drops a book.
The imprint of your invisible body
glitters in the dust on the floor.

Story of the Invisible Child

The invisible child tells a story.
The hum on her lips makes me glow
with the light of the resurrected.

She pulls creatures from the earth.
I sprout leaves.

Wake up.
There has been a fire but I'm not burned.

It takes years to walk through my house
because I've grown roots, and I notice everything—
blue and yellow bowl my wife bought
in Saint Augustine—
three-foot vase with the half-faces
of sun and moon, and a dish of blue crystals
we smudged with sage.

I could tell you everything I didn't notice
before the fire, before the strange child
whispered in my ear, but I can only hum
and you would not understand me.

Touch of the Invisible Child

Only children know how to disappear.

Hear that?
The invisible child walks through town
making us vanish.

She slips into each house
humming like a winged creature
waiting at the edge of a pond
on a summer night.

Nothing is beyond her reach.

Sit at night beneath a tree in a heap of leaves
and as gradual as a fiery season under the moon,
you're gone.

Twilight's Grove

I'm a boy who sits with an old man
beneath poplars
looking out at rows of mint and basil.
Pails of storm water
blue in the sun,
which sinks behind crows
atop a fence.

Out there
children twirl bicycle rims,
blood brothers
by flash of glass in their palms.
I sit on this bench
old as rain, the smell
of earth after it storms.

It's never cold.

The history of the old man
is told by dead leaves
swirling in the water.
We talk about those who
have yet to show up,
eat apple slices soaked in wine,
burn the skin of tangerines.

Dust in acres of light.
The moon quartered on a string.

Evening is a slow train into night
arrives at the bell of dark.

My father stands at a fountain,
his blue eyes seem to remember
something he was about to say
a long time ago.

After the Twining

Girls become women
after they have been kissed
by lightning.
Bound together
by silk of a falling star,
boy and girl skip
stones across a pond.

This is written in books.

Something hums between them.
Vines curl around their ankles.
The boy points to the sky.
A spark flares at the girl's lips.

They walk to the edge
of each page in a thousand books
about the beginning of the world.

Saints of Electrocution

I read a short story about a woman who was hit by lightning and for the rest of her life she was able to perform small miracles. Her hands were always hot. She met a man who had also been struck, and when they made love small birds twirled from their bodies. Afterward her house smelled of charcoal and lavender, green and violet blooms crisscrossed their flesh in a factual network of iridescent trees.

I worked in a factory assembling transformers, testing them with bursts of voltage. I'd dial the juice up or down based on the number of red wires. Some were a few inches long, others a couple of feet. Sometimes one of them touched my lap or wrist. The jolt threw me off the bench. If you saw me naked, you'd see tattoos of angry angels where I was kissed and burned.

The Meeting

After the meeting ended,
after the coffee and cigarettes,
an announcement could be made.
For years the majority held
the same opinion.
Their minds were made up.

But before those who disagreed
could burn homes,
send children to a faraway village,
the decision was kept mum
until they could disconnect the town
from the outside world.

They deliberated whether to tell
anyone anything at all.
In the end, they thought it best
not to say a word.

The Patriot

It was a time
when bodies long buried
in vast tombs under the villages
rose like decaying angels
with all but their eyes.

Eliot escaped the camps,
jumped a train,
fled to a sparse stand of trees.

But not for long.
He had stolen a rune from a festival tent.

Accused of having knowledge
about the working of things,
he was the first to wake up surrounded,
the first to disappear.

After the Blast

I went out for a loaf of bread. A pack of Lucky Strikes. President Kennedy said the Soviets would not be permitted to keep missiles on Cuba. And then I ran out of gas. I ran out of gas while taking a shortcut through a field where I once made love under a tree. The sun exploded, an egg breaking in the middle of a sizzling pan. Maybe I screamed. Is anything left? When the world shakes that much everything falls over like toy soldiers in a living room storm. I had a woman. I married a girl from a town that doesn't exist. I can't remember her name. I can't remember mine. Were there children? What of the children? Maybe there was a boy or girl, who ran to me when I came home. But who gets to go home when the world is smoke in the eyes of god?

I kept walking.

My name is stuck inside me like a leaf in the mouth of a man dead three days along the banks of a river. A man without fingerprints whose wallet is a washed-out life. How long have I been here? How long have I been a ghost in the middle of the world?

Alphabetical Disorder

What if it has been there all along, the perfect poem, bits of lines, little sparks from the night sky scattered across abandoned pages? A poem quickened from an alphabet learned from a barefoot lady who glowed like ice and sunlight on the other side of the fence in my back yard?

My sister crumpled each page of my hieroglyphics, my left-handed runes, showed me the cold and lonely A, the gorged-on-meat B, and the silk math of C. I wrote them backward, right to left trying to capture the long hum from Cassiopeia, needing to hear the lady's voice, trying to be true to her cold feet of love.

The New Language

This how it begins.
Every letter is replaced
with an odd symbol,
a lingual virus
passed down from builders of Babel.
DNA goes awry,
double helix of AGTACG rearranged,
and instead of George Jetson
you become Gort.
You understand zeros and ones
but not the face of Robert Frost.

I read a story about an old woman
with a brain tumor who could not speak.
She had written thousands of letters
on hundreds of index cards—OFWAIHHBTN,
which was decoded years after she died—
Our Father Who Art In Heaven
Hallowed Be Thy Name.
You fear you'll be replaced
by something with dead eyes.

Write to a future you'll never see,
send it off like a prayer,
send it to a god that never knew your name.
Sail it.   Sail it on a paper plane
from the tallest tower in the world.

Done in Chalk

after El Fugitivo 1947 by Gabriel Figueroa

None realize that they are chalk
until they try to traverse the end
of the page and my blue coffee cup.

That they have lived so richly among
the arches of Central American churches
and the way baskets make shadows

against the jugs and walls of the plaza
only adds to their perplexed amazement
and finally, to their frustration.

Who would've believed, they must think,
that they were recently created by
a woman with a few sticks of chalk

colorful as they are, and that one
day they would reach the end
of their questions so completely?

Tower of Myth

What if the tower fell and took the stars? People line up, touch cold gravity, press ears against it to hear its last bell. Villagers from the other side of the fence arrive with rope and pulleys. The architect goes to a drafting table, unrolls blueprints which have already begun to disappear in his hands. Someone steals a piece of the obelisk walks off into the woods. In the distance banners proclaim a warning in symbols nobody's ever seen. A storm brews. A child sits on the roof of a farmhouse writing down everything she sees.

Birth of Myth

Days of sitting around with friends
each telling stories of villages
that though they did not exist
are true in the telling.

One friend told of hooded, shoving crowds,
another of nine women
all of them very quiet.

I spoke of a place
the day I was born,
pulled from a goddess
surrounded by soldiers.

My friends believed,
wrote down my words,
all of us wrote down
stories we told in languages we created.

We became what we wanted
and needed to be—
hero or dragon—
rising from a story of our own making.

Click

Somebody somewhere made a mistake
or willingly uncorked the test tube
containing the end of the world.
You saw it coming,
stole blueprints
from tombs under cathedrals
hoping that some day
after the dead have stopped rising
a surviving architect
might rebuild the world.
You did what any atheist would do—
walked through museums with a camera
saving the faces of Mao, Marilyn
and The Last Supper
for what comes after the cannibals.

Blueprints

Structured clean lines,
measured, delicate as morning light
when the sky, still drunk with the moon,
is speckled with birds.

A man draws with calibrated instruments,
slices lines thin and purple as veins,
traces boundaries linear as history,
marks exits, doors.

A cool silence of baby steps,
a final walk through the kitchen
before moving out
makes room for moving in.

Polished equations, elegant sums
certify that load-bearing walls
will hold skylights,
fans above a rhythm of rooms
where love will be made,
where days will etch
across our bodies like sundials.

This is a wizard's spell
cast by pen and wires,
pipes, footsteps, and sawhorses,
a man dreaming in blue geometry.

Once, I stepped into a room
where an architect leaned at a drafting table,
one hand holding a scrolled end,
the other flat down leaving prints.

I see it still—afternoon light easing
him into existence as if at any moment,
stunned and perfect,
he'll wake.

Gorgeous

The squares in this painting
could be burnt houses.
This oval, the last yellow melon
of a never-ending summer.
Circles outlined in charcoal
possess something holy
as if an angel climbed down
a ladder and touched them
with cold tears or whispered
something so full of sighs
it turned their eyes
to dull green stones,
which they carry
like messages to someone
not in the frame.
To cool down the fiery torment
in the bright acrylic
the shade of mango trees
drench oblong women
or guitars, which lean toward
the center of the canvas
where corners of triangles meet.
Diagonal lines bear the weight
of hard days and light,
I think they are tired soldiers,
exiled poets or one-eyed children
who have no sorrow,
or too much of it.
They've had enough of our world,
and so they wear us down
with their delicious clichés.

Spice

Your old wife
sets a plate before you
at the evening table,
looks, smells
as it always has,
but this time
look at her eyes,
they will not meet yours.
An apple slice
mellows in the wine,
there is a face in it.
Something in the broth
in your spoon
could only have come
from a faraway place.

Push back the meal.

Let birds appear on your lips.
Take daylight from your pocket
like an old timepiece
to tick a way out.
Tell the woman to look you
dead in the eyes.

Don't Blink

I sit on the other side of the room,
wondering if it'll move.

Won't listen to the coo and warble
of its make-believe.

And while my heart
is a little less free when it does moves,
I adore the mobility of it.

I wake to learn
it has always been
attached to my sleep.
All those dreams about flying.
All that sudden lifting off the ground.

No sense fighting.
Eventually the music,
if that's what it is,
lulls me into making friends with it.
I invite it in.
It needs me to sustain itself,
but I don't know that,
not until it's too late.

I only know the fairy tale
I only know the myth.
It's everywhere.

It knew my name before I was born.

Spark's Shadow

Here – you can have it.
Be sure it doesn't get loose,
else it'll smudge the air
with moonlight haze,
infect you with evening star's lullaby.
Once you fall under its spell
there's only one way
to bring the fever down—
place it in a bowl of water,
chant a rhyme.
When the heat comes down,
decorate your house
with a hundred candles.
It'll get hungry—
feed it cinnamon and rose petals.
When it starts to turn red,
strum a guitar until it mellows
to the pale yellow of Italian villages.
After being amused
by its ability to mimic language,
put it in a cigar box
with a tuning fork,
place it under the bed
of a friend with a note
that says Here –
you can have it.
Be sure it doesn't get loose.

Oboe

The oboe plays
whenever arrow pierces heel,
that grey hour
waiting for a child to die,
plays when something falls,
weaving its long breath
between white space
and black event.

Spill coins and the oboe
starts its forlorn affair,
comes out of the blue
at graveyards
among black umbrellas.

The oboe is heard in trees
just after sundown
on a day
when something glorious burns.

When one hears the oboe,
one walks in fog.

Evening of Metronomes

The gods dream of apricots and swans. He dreams of music, a kind of flute music curling around the white heads of lilies. He lounges in a hammock a body full of clouds. Fireflies dot the air with amber winks. Crows settle in magnolia trees. A woman in the window glistens, slippery as a wet mango should a man come to touch her shoulder. Then in the kind of twilight that tins the world, he whistles though none but the parrots can hear him.

Revenge of the Genie

I am a genie
uncorked by a demon
who whispers in my ear
that anything is possible—
Raise the dead, transfer money
from rich to poor.
Yet, I am just a regular Joe
dunking a doughnut in my coffee.
Still, I'm mocked by gruff truck drivers,
gritty waitresses jerking thumbs
at my large ruby ring,
billowing green robe and
lop-sided turban.

I am an angry genie
living in the back yard
of a feeble astronomer.
Sleep in his wheelbarrow.
Each night I sprinkle dead stardust,
appear in dreams all over town.

Revenge of the Atheist

What if you got drastic
about teaching the gods a lesson?
Tired of prayer, sacrifice,
kneeling in silence,
all that stuff about sin,
you gather pieces
of those sharp days
when somebody died young
while you sat with a bowed head.
You've had enough.
Curse Zeus and Jesus,
Jehovah and Thor.
Mix a batch of bile.
Take it to those who claim
they've been healed
by the laying-on of hands,
pour it down their throats.
They are to blame —
delusional Believers
who spew that manifesto
of cures for some,
Hell for others.
Set them on fire,
let the smoke of their bones
be a warning to those wizards
in the sky—It won't be long—
you're coming for them next.

Tea for One

What if you're an evangelist
whose faith cannot be shaken?
Your wife and children
betray and deny you.
Still, you shine
like a crucifix in darkness.

But what if your followers abandon you?

When you came to this town
nonbelievers were drawn to your
contagious belief,
went with you to the river.
But now weeds of disillusionment
grow rough, doubt infected
with old habits return.
The humble who believed in salvation,
turn foul with rot.
They want their money back.
Job tells you to salt your wounds,
bear any stone.
Jesus will hear and bless you.

What if everyone in your life
does not pass that test?
Will you ask for a cup of forgetfulness?

What if that is your only reward?

The Colony

In the dream lions tell you a story—
                        You are mirage—

You will not be born for another two thousand years

You walk with a handful of coins

to a stone path meandering down to a cave

You have been here before

The stars—silver blood after fresh kill

You find yourself among the unfortunate

If you hurry you can make it to the hill

If it's not too late you can catch the Savior

just before he tears himself from the cross

Static from Heaven

There they are: unreal faces
with eyes looking out
from rectangle hell,
not knowing they exist
as electronic ones and zeros
housed inside a screen.
They can never know
who fathered them
or their mother's
silver technology
that fierce digital stream
at the speed of light
with all the colors of god.

What child has not
tapped that screen
and tried to tell them
they are trapped?
The best of them believe
they sometimes have dinner
at famous cafes in Los Angeles
where fans bring them
napkins to autograph.
Bette Davis has
an electric signature
and eats her soup
without a care in the world.
Better she believe
it's all for her.
Let her have her infamy.
Let them all glow in the dark

on nights such as this.
Let them believe they are real.

Mirror People

I arrive when the sun dusts the world with a burning feather, carry a burlap sack

of broken mirrors. Written in moonlight on each shard it says—*Enter here.*

Watch your step. I've carried the sack for so long I can't remember who gave

it to me after taking the oath to faithfully bring it to girls sleeping beneath trees,

soldiers at prayer in trenches, anyone who's ever needed something more than

light to see in the dark. But I must hurry. It's getting late. They are at their mirrors.

They believe I can let them in.

Girl Who Gets Gifts from Birds

Erasure poem from an online Feb. 2015 BBC News article by writer and broadcaster Katy Sewall.

This is her most precious collection: small pieces of brown glass worn smooth by the sea, a broken light bulb, miniature silver ball, blue paper clip, yellow bead, faded black piece of foam, blue Lego piece sitting on the edge of the birdbath. Each item a gift given to her by crows. Sometimes they give the kind of presents they would give to their mate — dead baby birds. This object is one of her favorites: a heavily rusted screw she prefers not to touch. You don't see a crow carrying a screw unless it's trying to build its house. Gabi's relationship with crows began accidentally, a kind of transformation. They understand each other's signals. The crows were watching her.

Aunt Angelina's Prophecy

You will go down to the sea as morning breaks to remember your mother's hands

After she dies you will watch someone plant lilacs in dark soil. It will be

easy to fall asleep. A woman who will love the sound of your voice will hum all

her life as she wipes her face to sad, beautiful music someone in your family,

Angelina, who ran away with gypsies after the war stealing colored beads

with which your grandmother made necklaces and rings, will never come home.

Those beads scattered light on the cherry wood bureau in a feast of red and

indigo orbs. Even now, you hear that wonderful clock ticking. You will live a

long life intimate with Fuseli and the symmetry of vulvas. All your life you will

crave raw silk, winter tangerines. Only the nacreous light around women can

heal you, only the smell of old guitars. As a child you spent a summer afraid to

*climb down from a tree. You will dream about that for
forty years. I see a house*

*with a grape arbor, old men playing bocce. A birdbath and
statue of Mary*

*blackened by rain. Beware the stranger whose eyes greet you
like rare orchids.*

*She will come to you underneath an umbrella, her face and
hands deep in its shade.*

The Contraption

You invent a gizmo
designed to trap cosmic particles
that might tell us something
about the possibility of intelligent life
out in the stars.

What if it doesn't work?

Tap the silly thing attached to your head
like rabbit ears on a snowy TV, but nada.
It falls to an icy sidewalk
in front of your house
during an arctic vortex
and suddenly you hear something—

trapped sound caught in spiders' webs
all over the world—
conversations of thieves and sleepwalkers,
Morse code and the chirping of birds
extinct for a hundred years.

You hear the sound of chalk
on Einstein's blackboard,
Mary Shelley's story as it left her lips
that night in front of the fire.
But you are the only soul who can hear it.

The Machine

He gathers everybody in the room, tells them to talk while he sets things up. Turns the lights low before assembling the odd contraption. Everyone looks around for chairs. With hands in pockets or pulling at chains, they murmur, shrug. A few of them lean over as he pushes a black rod into a green component, ask questions. But he nods quickly pretending not to understand a word. Finally the monstrosity is complete. He plugs it in.

Everybody stops talking.

Somebody faints.

The Box

You put things in a box behind a wall in a house you lived in. You meant to collect what was inside. Wrote yourself a note. But years have gone by. You have moved away. What was inside? Birds' wings. Lightning glass. Peach pits from an afternoon with your grandfather catching pollywogs down by the stream. Starlight and Romans. If only you remembered to go back, the girl who spiked your heart on her wicked smile would've fallen in love with you. You'd have children with white silk hair, eyes blue enough to melt snow. But you cannot go back. You've never lived in that house. There was no box.

The Town

Several of them stood around the well
where girls sold flower bracelets.
After the sun went down we could hear dogs,
women. Nobody knew what to do.
Somebody took a shovel outside
said he was going to bury his wife,
instead hit one of them in the face.

The Girl on the Roof

She can only sing on the way down.

Birds that once helped her embroider a gown

slice little ribbons of blood from her cheek.

Evening's cool bronze flickers

like a burnt fairy tale in the windows of her face.

Fairies have stopped glowing in the dark,

night has come on a violet wish.

She believes there will be a song so sweet

earth will kiss her goodnight,

a young man will bring her the lost slipper

of a life she almost lived.

She throws her pumps at a man on a ladder,

not a boy-prince with a sonnet on his lips.

Her body is a paper lantern.

The moon says burn it, throw it from the roof,

the coach and horses will not stop here.

Lady in the Yellow Summer Dress

I will die here, he says
to the woman next to him
who looks out the window.
She makes no gesture
as the town, and its local history,
blurs by. Architects who designed
green and pink art deco
are long gone. I have lived here
all my life, he says, and the woman
shuts her eyes expecting his hand
to accidentally touch her knee
but he only stares, she can feel it,
stares at the silent flicker
of buildings catching the afternoon
in its glass, catching the moving world,
blinding him with old geometry.
And then only the sound of the rumbling bus.
The lady dreams of a girl
who raises parakeets by the Mediterranean Sea,
dances with her father in a gypsy village
who play violins in the rain.
She grows up without ever having to leave,
and the birds, soft and yellow
as the sun in their cage, never die.

Catching Angels

Everything becomes what you want it to be in the dark.
A cat is a clock ticking on your bed.

Old radio dial glows with secret codes
from Purgatory or Russia.
Angels skate on edges of the Milky Way.

My grandmother once told me to put blue crystals
on a window sill to trap the stars.

And now the Little Dipper is burning.
The Little Dipper is falling.

Something delirious struggles in the window.

Angel's Song

She sings to you
from across the twilight
of long ago and not yet.
Each morning light makes air
a tuning fork of color.
She plucks a feather from her wing.
You float above a town
made of short stories.
There is a song in your head.
This is where you belong,
floating like a sigh
above the trees.
When your feet touch ground
you wake to feathers
leading to a crib
where an infant sleeps
beneath a blanket of murmurs.
Open your eyes.
This is the day you are born.

Rain

Catch rain in colored bottles, place them on the sill. Remember a prayer, the talking silence of hands, the need to fill things with water, because this is the story of rain on a day when screen doors fill with shadows, when a dog circles his world before it pours. Put out pails, clay vessels and fruit jars. Cut the world with broken glass. Even if there is no god, the sound of someone crying in a house with a broken skylight is holy. You are a woman at a window filled with old light, tears on your face. A field burns with sudden hail, the madness of falling stars.

Windows

I collect windows in a bottle, and as you might expect, windows are the same everywhere. Mostly. The first one, I stole from the Grand Canyon, kept it in the pocket of my blue jeans where it squirmed real good trying to get out. When I got home, I realized I had no place to keep it, so I put it in this bottle. Sure it tried to escape. Tricky, windows. They're so clear, hard to see in glass, and after my thumb got bit a few times, or cut—you can't tell with windows—I put in a nice snug cork. The Grand Canyon bumps and clicks against what seems like infinite out, but after a while it knows it ain't going nowhere. At first, I loved to hold the bottle up to my bedroom window, you know, to see it better, but it was harder, had to squint, the Grand Canyon almost disappeared, plus being held up to the light, it got all riled up again. Eventually, I learned the best way to see it was to wait for the sun to set, when the stars appear up there, you put the bottle closer to them by taking it outside, let it sit there on the grass awhile to absorb the light. After an hour or two, like sun-ripened tea, the window mellows and glows a little. Once I saw the Little Dipper in it shining like a dull butter knife on an old wooden table. After that night, I said to myself, maybe I can find more windows and keep them in the bottle, you know, sort of a menagerie of windows from all over the place. So when I went to the top of the Sears Tower in Chicago, I took a window, when I visited Rome, I took a window from one of the arches in the Coliseum. That's a good one. Sometimes you can see lions and Roman soldiers in the starlight. By the way, you can't put the bottle under the moon, it's too powerful, moonlight drowns windows so all you see is a bottle of light; there's no pictures in it. I've been collecting windows for a long time now and I've snuck some from museums, one from the Eiffel Tower, and

I've got windows from Machu Picchu, a café in Soho, and one from a porno theater in New Orleans, but I think I like the Grand Canyon window best. Maybe because it's my first. Also, it makes me feel like I'm on the edge of something too big to talk about, like I'm about to fly.

Notes

"Festival of Dangerous Ideas" is "an annual event presented by Sydney Opera House and The Ethics Centre that brings leading thinkers and culture creators from around Australia and the world to discuss and debate some of the most important issues of our time".—- Wikipedia

"Thirty-foot burning man of straw" references Burning Man

"red meat, heads and limbs of dolls" references The Beatles original Capitol Records American LP cover "The Beatles Yesterday and Today"

"Marco Polo" is a shout-out to Italo Calvino's wonderful book *Invisible cities*

"old man juggles…" foreshadows all coming references in the collection to **"The Sleep Talker,"** this includes all mention of wizards and professors

In **"The Sleep Taker"** "the old professor" — I envision The Sleep Talker as Albert Einstein

"*I see myself in the shock-work of stars*" is after Walt Whitman

"a boy with a girl in the woods sprinkling breadcrumbs" … references Hansel & Gretel while the next line "or a man in Vienna making a puppet out of wood" references Gepetto of "Pinocchio," and foreshadows the poem "Gepetto's Smile" The original intent of this collection was for it to be a book of poetic fables or fairy tales. The original title was simply *Fables*

"Mr. Zootageek" comes from a story my grandmother told about a shoemaker in Italy who abducted "bad" children. I've spelled his name phonetically. I don't know the correct spelling as my grandmother was illiterate and is long gone.

"Consuelo Maldonado Returns," Maldonado was a girl in junior high school whom I liked. I had a dream about her almost 50 years later. We never spoke, and she never knew me.

"Man Who Teaches Children to Fly" could also be a wizard and is another magical idea. It foreshadows other poems in the collection about magical or strange children all of whom -boy or girl- could be the boy who enters the Festival in the first poem.

"Escape" was written after I had walked through a local museum jotting down the titles of works of art on display. There are one or two titles I invented for the poem. The second stanza references the 1974 sci-fi film "Phase IV".

"Library of Imaginary Books" references the novel *The Shadow of the Wind* by Carlos Ruiz Zafron. It's opening line is "I still remember the day my father took me to the Cemetery of Forgotten Books..." and I knew I had to write this poem. Also, I've always fantasized sleeping overnight in a library or bookstore.

All the "child" references in the three **"Invisible Child"** poems poems are also the boy—or girl—who has entered the Festival. They are interchangeable with all reference to other children and the "I" in many of other poems in the collection.

In **"Touch of the Invisible Child"** the line "A walk through my house/takes a few years/because instead of feet," ... is a re-write of a line in a poem by Michael Hettich.

"Saints of Electrocution" references a short story I'd read—title now forgotten—about a woman who was struck by lightning and then was able to heal people.

In **"The Patriot"** the character Eliot was a homeless man I befriended, who acted outlandishly and strange when approached by police or strangers. Eventually, he let his game face down with me and I learned he was a very intelligent man who had an encyclopedic knowledge of jazz and all things New York City. He slept under the stairwell of the office building I worked in the 1990s. Several years later I heard he was found dead.

"After the Blast" is an ekphrastic piece. The image was an old 1960s era car in the middle of a field near one dead tree.

Most of the original versions of the poems in this collection began with the prompt "What if," **"Alphabetical Disorder"** retains the "What if" as the opening. It also references an idea I had to go back through some old workshopped poems (led by Carolyn Forche, Denise Duhamel, Yehuda Amichai and others) and cherry pick lines they highlighted as being worthy or to be cut and putting them on paper to form a found poem. The poem also refers to "a barefoot lady who glowed like ice and sunlight on the other side of the fence in my back yard," which was either a dream or a vision I had at 4 years old. This woman appears in other poems in *Festival*, "my hieroglyphics, my left-handed runes" references my earliest attempts at writing, again, after the dream or vision of the lady in my back yard. I filled pages of gibberish and scribbles until my older sister taught me the ABCs, which I wrote backward being left-handed.

In "**The New Language**," the line "block letters on hundreds of index cards—OFWAIHHBTN," is a true story about a woman who had a brain tumor and wrote those letters on cards. Her children finally figured out what the letters represented after she died. George Jetson was a cartoon character in the 1960s TV series "The Jetsons," about a family living in the future where cars flew and each home had a robot. Gort is the name of the robot in the 1950s classic Sci-Fi film "The Day The World Stood Still".

In "**Birth of Myth**," "Days of sitting around with friends" and "hooded, shoving crowds" are from "Orpheus Alone" by Mark Strand; "Nine women all of them very quiet," is from "Apollo Takes Charge of His Muses" by A.E. Stallings, which were prompts given in a workshop by Julie Marie Wade.

"**Gorgeous**," came about after my wife and I visited a gallery featuring an artist whose work was overwhelmingly "gorgeous," so by the time we viewed the 20th piece or so, instead of feeling these were fabulous pieces, we felt oppressed by so much of the same shapes and colors.

In "**Aunt Angelina's Prophecy**," the character herself is based on my Aunt Angie, who lived most of her life with gypsies, telling

70

fortunes, traveling from town to town all over the country. According to her, she had been abducted, (she was living in a homeless shelter in the 1950s after her husband abandoned her) according to family, she ran off with a gypsy man with her three small children. She told of beatings by her husband and his mother when she tried to get back to our family. She once told me that in the gypsy way of life, "American" women or wives, were made to serve the mother-in-law, cooking and cleaning etc.

"Rain" is from an abandoned chapbook collection of poems about or inspired by The Beatles.

Acknowledgements

The author would like to thank the editors of the following literary magazines journals and presses, in print and online, in which these poems, or versions of them, first appeared:

NightBallet Press for the chapbook *The Sleep Talker* in which the following poems appeared: "The Sleep Talker", "Blueprints", "Library of Imaginary Books", History of the Invisible Child", "Touch of the Invisible Child", "Story of the Invisible Child", "Alphabetical Disorder" (as "Runes"), "Catching Angels", "Gorgeous" (as "Gorged on Gorgeous"), "Mirror People", "Static from Heaven", "Revenge of the Atheist", "Revenge of the Invisible Man", "Revenge of the Genie", "Strangers in a Grove", "Twilight's Grove", "The Beginning of Daydreams", "The Contraption", "Windows" and "The Man Who Teaches Children to Fly".

Fairy Tale Review for "Windows" (as Fable XIX) and "Lost Boy" (as Fable IX).

"The Sleep Talker," "Spark's Shadow" and a slightly different version of "Blueprints" were anthologized in *Twice Upon a Time* (Kind of Hurricane Press).

Danse Macabre Literary Journal for alternate versions of "The Return of Consuelo Moldonado" and "Mr. Zootageek".

Blotterature for "Gepetto's Smile".

2River View for "The Angel's Song", "Spice", "Don't Blink" and "Saints of Electrocution".

Blueshift Journal for "The Girl Who Gets Gifts from Birds".

Half Tones to Jubilee for "Aunt Angelina's Prophecy" (as "The Fortuneteller").

The Potomac for "The Meeting" and "Click".

Ginger Bread House for "Tower of Myth".

Chiron Review for "The Contraption," "The Girl on the Roof" and "Catching Angels".

Blue Fifth Review for "The Box".

Poetrybay for "Done in Chalk" and "Rain" (as "Green Bottle in the Window").

Poet Lore for "Neo".

About the Author

Lenny DellaRocca is founder and co-publisher of *South Florida Poetry Journal (SoFloPoJo)* and *Interview With A Poet*, both at southfloridapoetryjournal.com. His poems appear in *Poet Lore, Poetrybay, 2River view, Fairy Tale Review, Chiron Review, Seattle Review, POEM, Laurel Review, Apalachee Review, Sun Dog, Gulf Stream Magazine, Mad Hat, Wisconsin Review, The Potomac* and *Nimrod*. He is a Pushcart Prize nominee. He has three collections of poetry: *The Sleep Talker* (Night Ballet Press), and *Blood and Gypsies* (Anaphora Press), and *Things I See in the Fire*, winner of the 2017 Yellow Jacket Chapbook contest (Yellow Jacket press).

About the Press

UNSOLICITED PRESS is a small press based in the Pacific Northwest. The press is operated by outstanding, experience volunteer editors, marketers, and cover designers dedicated to producing high-quality poetry, fiction, and creative non-fiction. Unsolicited Press was established in 2012 with little more than a strong drive — in the years since, it has grown into a well-oiled machine. You can learn more at www.unsolicitedpress.com.

www.ingramcontent.com/pod-product-compliance
Lightning Source LLC
Chambersburg PA
CBHW020129130526
44591CB00032B/580